When You Get Here

When You Get Here

Poems by

Shutta Crum

Cover art by Nathan Dumlao at Unsplash.com

Cover design by Shay Culligan

ISBN: 978-1-950462-86-5

Kelsay Books Inc.

kelsaybooks.com

502 S 1040 E, A119
American Fork, Utah 84003

for Gerry, always. . .

Acknowledgments

What wonders the love of poetry has brought to my life. Through poetry I met my husband who was an assisting editor of a small press poetry journal. He came to me with two amazing children through whom I acquired the deliciousness of grandchildren. Poetry has also brought me many life-long friends who have listened to and critiqued some of the poems in this volume. Among them is my first writing instructor Fred Wolven, a fantastic poet and an editor of the online AAR2. I owe you so much! Thank you, Fred. And thanks to the endurance of a fantastic poetry group that includes Chris Lord, Don Hewlett, Mike Long, Jayne Black, Marilyn Churchill, Jay Platt, Sue Budin and John Lloyd. What stalwarts you all are for hanging in there with me. Bless you. In addition, I must thank the members of my Florida writers' group who encouraged me to submit this manuscript. Also, I owe a big thank you to Chris Lord and Betsy Baier for their eagle eyes in proofreading this manuscript. Finally, as always, thank you to Gerry Clark my husband, and to my family for understanding how much seeing the world through the lens of poetry means to me—even if my take on things is sometimes a little wonky.

Many thanks to the publications my poems have appeared in over the years. They include:

AAR2 (online Ann Arbor Review): "Coming Into Your Life—Driving Directions for My Daughter," "When You Get Here—Driving Directions for My Son," "How to Walk Well in the World," "Uphill," "Either Direction," "The Path Through the Palms," "Childhood," "The Gift," "Some, Too Indifferent to Spring Winds," "Our Luminous Patient," "Translating Lines," "The Leaving Season," "Funeral Procession," "In the Heart's Land," "Love Poem for a Rainy Night," and "Marriage Bed."

Wayne Literary Review: "The Visitor."

Huron Valley Review: "Watching You Sleep."

Current Magazine: "You Can Have It Back."

Ann Arbor (W)rites: "A Philosophy of Luminescence."

Literary Life: "Summer Portrait."

Writers Reading at Sweetwaters: "Father's Cupboard."

Stoneboat Literary: "A Life Bespoke."

Contents

Driving Directions

From My Own Wilderness

after Loren Eiseley

From this vantage point
I can see down the road
through the marsh.
It is a hazardous route, trod deeply
through the murk of history.
Things have fallen by the wayside
to become curiosities in some far time.
Today the light is green, moss damp,
and thick with voices.
It is here that I'll await you: oh, beloved one.
Whether you come winged, or hoofed,
finned or tailed, or even, rooted.
In my time there are bones and
memories that are imprecise.
They fit together only with willful
abandon. So, I have no doubt
that a new and luminously crafted you
will one day walk this road.
Then I shall welcome you from
my own wilderness—literate only
in the language of long-ago twilights.

Coming into Your Life: Driving Directions for My Daughter

for Jennifer

Go! Take the keys to the truck.
Wave as you pull out of the drive.
Don't worry that street signs are
blank; claim each deserted crossroad
as your own. And when you get to a
country that needs your truths
turn right, then right again.

Stop often and ask for directions.
Talk with your hands. Laugh
when you sprawl upon the grass
and feel the Earth traveling, too.

In small towns listen to the women
who stare out windows. Don't strand
yourself with zealots upon the curb of
one idea. They have their own
pilgrimages to make.

Move! Pinch off little pieces of your
heart and besparkle the footprints
you leave behind. It hurts, but it is a
sacred act.

Drive down farm lanes. Steal a peach.
Not a perfect one—take the one that
nestles against your skin with the
familiarity of home. Eat it on a hilltop
with the sun on your face.

Be sure to tell the man you've met
that he is beautiful. Then, when the
sorrel-colored bellies of leaves brush
your skin, make love.

When you are heavy with child,
come home. We will pick wild berries
and kiss each other with summer-
stained lips.

And the child in you will move.

When You Get Here: Driving Directions for My Son

for Geoff

Turn off your GPS.
Travel where gravel pings
the underside of your car,
where you can smell manure
on farm fields. Allow the wind
to ride shotgun. Let it blow away
maps and reminders. Go.

Don't take the first road,
or the second. Wait until afternoon
shadows lengthen, then drive
toward the last glimmerings
of the day. When small animals
prepare for night—turn.

By the lake stop to admire fathers
carrying their sleepy young
home in the twilight. Watch
wet beach towels trail in the dirt.
Smell the weedy damp of the lake.
When they've all crossed the road
put on your blinker, and wait until
the white dog has trotted safely over.

Spend the night someplace
where cookies are served.
In the morning, ask directions
of the old man sweeping the drive.
Follow them precisely—in reverse.
Don't stop for gas. Drive through fields
of wheat, let it push your car along.

Tell the companion you'll find
that she is beautiful. Then . . .
when you arrive, we'll have wine
bottled in the year you were born,
and pears—oddly shaped, but plucked
from a tree that's been waiting for you
to get here.

How to Walk Well in the World

1.

Step softly when storefronts are still groggy with sleep.
They have not blinked fully into life and can be surly
this early in the morning. Slip between the defenses
of their silent, crossed streets. Rescue wind-tossed
sentences blown against your shins. There are always
witnesses, even that yellow dog emerging from the alley.
He will be called on to testify.

2.

Whisper when you hear the cracked voices of weathered
men who have worked the earth. With or without their women,
they have sampled the colorings of time, can run their bruised
hands over the rust of old affairs, and know how to love
what is orphaned. They'll not welcome you with words.
One will spit. One will squint into the haze of a summer heavy
with the fullness of soybeans and daughters. Bow when they sweep
the dust from battered boxes, and mutter, "Sit."

3.

Be a guest in the foyers and parlors of others' lives.
Take your shoes off at the door and acknowledge grief.
Bring a casserole. Do not settle into armchairs. Quietly,
admire baby pictures, baseball trophies. Stand and lean
into each other. Do not talk. This is all that is required
to walk well in the world.

Uphill

Flex your knees.
Keep your hips loose, and lean in—
heartwise—to the incline.
Don't bother with looking back.
Breathe.
Find a dog to come along.
He will witness
without rebuke or blame.
Breathe deeper.
Let each footfall accept its fate.
When you're ready, look up.
See. There's the lost lamb
grazing in the high meadows
amid wild cicely.
Wait while she ruminates.
She'll want to confer upon the weather,
upon the elemental tide in the blood,
and upon the arcane geometry of sedges.
Sit a while. Breathe anise scented air.
Squint into blue distances.
A far river will wink knowingly.
A half-forgotten horizon will grace you
with forgiveness.
The lamb will wander again.
It is her nature. She is not ungrateful.

Either Direction

Do you remember the dream you had?
The one when you were eleven.
About the abandoned road—old tarmac
slumped across sunbaked fields.
And you beside it, in your mother's chenille robe
decorated with five pink roses. Remember?

You were standing amid chicory the color of sky.
Sweet clover and bindweed splayed over your bare feet.
You were singing that silly song: *The ants go marching
one by one. Hoorah! Hoorah!*

You pressed your toe into a soft ribbon of tar.
The seal of a promise. The ants, the chicory—
silent witnesses. Do you remember that dream?
The one when you were nine. Or maybe you were seven.
The one you never told a soul about. I do. I remember it.

This is what I want to tell you about your dream:
go either direction—the road is yours. Yours and the ants.
The sweetness of clover will trail behind.
One by one, or two by two—the road knows the way.
It's been dreaming of you, a pilgrim bearing roses.
It's waited for you through long sun-drenched days
and moon-fogged nights with the patience of an old dog.

The Path through the Palms

The path through the palms
is sandy and hot. It dips
into hollows and tracks cleverly
over roots and the ghosts of roots.
Disorderly

and unapologetic; yet I think
it will serve you, my praise-singing
child caught up in mystery.
Let your feet knead the old path—
blistery

with memory. Where does it lead?
That is not important now. But see,
it narrows in a flurry
of furthering itself. If you're coming,
hurry!

Roadside Attractions

Fern Hill Lost

after Dylan Thomas

Now as I was blindly young
and skipped through days sunbaked,
or galloped through the leaf-light green,
no troubles raked the land I ruled.
And no one there but they were righting
all that needed righting before ever I could grieve.

No troubles pooled;
for I was young and happy-hearted.
I wore my dappled days like jeweled gowns
bespoke, above a weave of mud-caked toes.
Time cartwheeled, laughing, just for me.
Or so I thought.

An elemental Eve—
Oh, I was flush with fairy moss so gladly worn,
and lost in plumpsom thoughts.
The backyard imps proclaimed me empress
for all I touched touched back with tenderness.
But I was young and blameless still.
The days, diaphanous, were not yet torn.
The hearts of those I met felt fat and full.

Yes, I was young and reigned beloved.
The windfall light had not yet dimmed.
My pact with autumn brimmed with gold.
What sense had I of ice-born truth?
What fear of winter's night-jacked breath?
Or time's cruel tooth?

Childhood

for John

In the greening fields
his mother is dancing.
She is brown-limbed and earthy-eyed.
Her beauty—a carnival
of cherry red ribbons.

She picks him up.
Her ribbons brush his cheek.
He clutches her sunlight-drenched hair
in his fat-fisted pagan hands.

He will hold her as long as he can.

The Gift

for Cal

Brown
slip of boy
come
bringing
that fistful
of sticks.

Catkins—
in first blush.

Imp of My Heart

for Brenda

I went looking for the right words,
seeking a poem for you, imp of my heart.

Found, instead, barefoot days and
a round face wreathed in a halo of mud.
Your two small hands holding tight
against a bare belly—bent—to keep back
an avalanche of giggles. Silly girl.

Found, instead, a big-girl room and
a large bed shared—your half, my half.
Our hands decreeing the invisible wall
inviolable between us. Then waking to find
the wall had grown moony as it cradled us.
Silly wall.

Found, instead, time had shaped a woman
and tested her strength. Those hands held
strong. Are still holding laughter. Silly time.

Found, instead, that I did not need to search
for a poem for you. You *are* my poem—always.
Imp of my heart. Silly sister.

Father's Cupboard

My father's cupboard—built by hand—
held baby food jars and Prince Albert Tobacco cans
full of nails or screws. And always, oily boxes
with torn labels too heavy for me to tip and peek into.
These were the secret things my father used
to hold the world together.

Committed these fifty years to the basement,
bracing the house I grew up in.
It was once Mom's kitchen cupboard.
Dad painted it smiling-teeth white and Kool-Aid red.
It sat near to bursting in the kitchen until banished
in favor of Danish modern.

This morning in the basement, jacking up
the kitchen floor above, it takes four to extract
the cupboard from the embrace of joists.
For the house is sagging now despite the stoic Danes,
despite Dad.

I brush away cobwebs, check all its porcelain knobs.
It is dripped with spilled paint—pink on red.
Perhaps the pink he used making a small table and chairs?
Or the pink of a dollhouse—almost forgotten. And sky blue.
Perhaps a birdhouse, or a project of my brother's?
Maybe the blue of the chair that sat in the yard
idly reflecting on the sky while I attended school,
met boys and fell in love.

My father's cupboard is scarred and anointed with color.
Until the very end we left it to its labors,
and only now wrest it from the grieving house.

Summer Portrait

There may have been an ice cube tray
smacked against the metal-rimmed
counter-top, the plonking of cubes
into jelly glasses, and a furious
crackling as ice fissured in lemonade.

There may have been the sough
of sullen air skulking through the dead
switch grass after she disappeared
through the door—her thin dress
a fleeting distraction for the dust.

There may have been kitchen chairs
carried out into the shade
of the crippled willow. And the Buick
may have been on blocks, beleaguered
by goldenrod and blue asters.

I don't recall if static
from the transistor radio masked
droning insects—or if she spoke at all.
But like the lacings of a cicada's husk,
there remains a small knot of memory.

The slap of pink flip-flops
across the hard-pack of the yard,
half-moons of watermelon on white plates,
and on our arms black seeds
in the sticky wash.

What He Brought Me

It appears at dinnertime
by my chipped yellow plate,
this gift of white quartz.
Oddly shaped,
it has no use—that I can see.
Perhaps it winks in the sunlight?
Or hypnotizes with its depths?

I pick it up and sit with it in my hand.
My grandchild watches,
lower lip sucked in.
Across his arched wrist—upright,
thin—a fragile vein pulses.

This tiny crystal mountain
has known time and forces
that would crush us in an instant.
And it will weather millennia, yet,
before it blows away in the wind—
even then . . .

I place it in the lamplight.
My grandchild rests his chin
on the table and stares into it,
seduced by the shine.

He is too innocent to pay homage
to the hard truth of this rock—
how breakable we are.

In a House above Which UFOs were Sighted in 1966

The rumble of a jet reverberates off low clouds.
I close my eyes and strain to hear,
cloaked within, stealthier sounds.

At my side there is the eddying churn of your breathing.
First the sibilant intake, then the buffaloing exhale.
And there—that's the cat alighting between us.
He takes two turns across the foot of our bed
complaining about his arthritis. Not a perfect landing.
Not . . . say . . . like the shimmery touch
of silver sliding through soybeans.

And surely that . . . Listen! Isn't that the maple tree
dropping a branch upon the roof?
Or the house planting itself deeper into the soil—
into land settled by honest Lutheran farmers.
Big, solid men. Plain speakers who offer travelers a beer.

By my bed lies the newspaper clipping.
Forty years ago, Washington experts said: swamp gas.
Surely, they knew how swamp gas graced
a German farmer's soy field like gossamer
and rose again in a fantasy of flickering lights
against moon-lit metal?
The farmers shook their heads. Muttered.
These unimaginative men knew what they saw—
plain as the honest dirt on their hands.

Tonight, the jet's rumblings have flattened out and moved off.
I stare out the bedroom window into the scintillescent dark.
Fireflies are bejeweling the maple tree as though expecting royalty.

Detours & Tolls

Some, Too Indifferent to Spring Winds

after Emily Dickinson

All things must rise—or die, it seems.
From darkness comes desire.
Or so glad Spring would have us think—
in Winter's wake, there's fire.

But I have not decided yet
who tells the truer tale.
Perhaps it's ice that kindles heat—
when pain's what we inhale.

For all that Spring does set ablaze,
it's Winter's craven turns
that brings us to our knees with grief,
ignites the heart, and burns.

The Visitor

The wolf has followed me onto the ice.
From the icicle-fringed portal
of my anorak I see, at times,
her shaggy coat. Snow-fog soft
and indistinct, or sudden, sharp,
and ice crusted. An apparition
perhaps. Grayer than the gray
of this night. Whiter than this veil
through which I push.

On the frozen lake I stake
my little yellow tent in the lee
of ice boulders, rigid and risen
in prayer. Its sides slap a futile
diatribe against the deafening wind.

In the breath-heated cocoon of my
dreams, the wolf paces before my tent.
I struggle through weight-burdened sleep,
imprisoning cloth, down bag,
and crystallized breath to find
the waking eye of consciousness—
the door in the dark. And I crawl out
groping for light and silence.

In the momentary calm of a large drift,
she greets me. By snowlight we are
nose to nose. She is wolf, not phantom—
the air about her stilled, warm.
She, more civilized than I.
I rock back on my haunches,

startled by the heat of her breath,
by the sudden lifting of the veil,
by the quelling of wind. So quickly.
I can hear—even my own stranded heart.

Slowly, I remove one glove.
Stretch out fingertips, aware
of my ill-mannered intention.
A forgivable sin, I hope. I . . .
Inhaling, the wind catches its breath.
The snowy veil drops, and she is gone.

I struggle, crawling back
through the grinding darkness.
My tent beating, once more, its frantic
tattoo in the outraged wind.
I curl in this cold cacophony—
knees to chest beneath what layers
I can muster in the necessary closeness.

And she comes again. The wolf
has followed me onto the ice. Here,
circling in my impatient dreams, she yearns
to lie down in the baptizing snow beside me.

A Philosophy of Luminescence

1.0: the slope of the glow curve*

You said there was beauty in the mathematical
choreography of proof. I closed my eyes
and saw signs and symbols cavorting on stage,
numbers colliding. They were stepping on toes,
leaping on the wrong beat, stopping to pull up
a stocking that had lost its elastic to the
string theorists in the audience. And staring
big-eyed from behind a curtain, a small decimal
point that refused to move.

You danced your hand through the air: *wave theory*.
I saw us riding the dorsal hump of a glowing curve.
Me, clutching its golden sides. You, whispering
thermoluminescence and igniting what simple dreams
I had. What I could not see were the calculations
of arc and temperature, or the allotting of duration—
all charted according to immutable laws.

1.1.0: a short life at room temperature

The night I wandered across campus,
I thought about our bodies: water and fire.
Our bones: calcium, phosphorus. After birth
we begin the process of decaying, carrying within
a dusty light. Phosphorescence, the light
of burial chambers.

Bombardment by particles creates heat, and light.
"Intensity," you said. But it also quickens the rot,
I argued. You conjectured that light is stable
at higher temperatures. I countered that Darwin
had cut off the heads of glowworms to excite their
luminescence. But irritated light does not last long.
In the end, he had a lot of dead bugs.

That's the trouble with experiments—
There's always garbage to clean up. And it
was becoming clear that there was not room
for anomalies in the elegant equation of your life.
One night, I did not come home—
in the name of science.

1.2.0: the density of light

Our marriage had reached a threshold
of numbers. Its specific gravity was charted.
And though confined light can behave as if
it has mass, its density is solely dependent
upon confinement. Finally, the impact
of trace impurities on light is complex.
You would move on to other experiments.
I would stumble about in the dark and
sometimes find myself in boneyards of memory.
There I would stop and run my hands
over the knobby turnings of phalanges
and mandibles. Then I would emerge to splay
my fingers and study the light remaining,
this glow on my palms.

I am no scientist, no theorist of quantum
innuendo, yet even I could see that this weakest
and oldest of light had the power to illuminate.
At an elemental level, all possibilities are possible.
So, I wiped my hands on my shirt and strode off,
the messy splotch down my front scribing a
shaky trajectory.

2.0: *the path described by a body moving*
under the action of given forces

Though it had been an inconclusive study,
there were numbers to catalog—pure data.
Years would pass. You would publish your findings.
Accolades would follow.

I, too, would write of it.

*(Some section headings: thanks to Heinz Anderle on
thermoluminescence,©1997.)*

Our Luminous Patient

All night we listened to the lunatic
fray—to the flailing skirmishes of
ragged words and ravaged limbs.
When we thought morning had finally
come, we threw open the door and the
moon staggered into our arms.

What was there to do but brace
ourselves against the good wood
of this house and shore-up the
ramparts in our father's room?
For we are bound by blood and the
glorious burnish of his long lustrous years.

And now—oh, how many nights
we barely sleep fearing our luminous
patient will rise to rage the length
of the house, will push aside our
ministering hands, will lift his fervid
face toward battle.

Oh, how many nights we barely sleep
knowing that we who love our father
will be re-marshaled to strip the
singed sheets from his bed, to bar the
door, and man the barricades.

So we lie awake, aquiver to the fading
champion next door—to any
benighted din heralding a new
campaign, another turn of the siege,
another tremulous surrender.

Yes, we will catch him up in our arms;
a sickle-shaped sliver of his old self—
pale, tested. And for a moment we will
steady the old soldier in his waning
course through our sky.

On the Dock at Crystal Lake, I Remember

for Dad, 1925-2008

"It's water, Dad. Drink."

The warped dock hosts a shadow—a reflected dock.
Bold light and dark slats skew on the waves,
like the twisting and untwisting of DNA.
Perhaps the two strands twined in this daughter—
lakeside summers and Dad keeping me afloat.

I study the cast-offs and fugitives below—
splayed clam shells, distressed glass, snails,
and almost translucent fingerlings that flick
small bodies beneath bulbous eyes.

Amid the dross of summer, bubbles have two reflections.
First, a white pinprick of light playing over sand.
Then a shadow twin—a bastard heir. Thief.

Stiffly, I rise from the dock. *Why is this?*
Our bodies are mostly water. I should roll, swirl,
easily swim into that dry country where,
holding his head up,
I lift water to my father's mouth.

Translating Lines

for the young victims of Nickel Mines: 10/2006

I drop my heels down the sharp edge
of concrete stretching the length
of hamstrings and tendons,
then trot into the fog. The western sky
is smudged with night. Pink is gashed
across the east.

The silver nib of a jet scribes another
contrail, crosshatching the sky.
Like me, it is headed toward the
morning star. Lights come on in
farmhouses. Sleepy drivers pass,
hugging the splayed edge of the road.

Uphill, I leave the fog and pass
the mounded body of a dead
woodchuck. Like a well-rounded
period, it is an ending readily
understood. The rustle in the dry corn
is more difficult to interpret.
The dying stalks have settled crookedly,
disordering the simple green march
of summer—the knowledge of lines.

I pass the horse farm, turn west
to return home—and see the moon.
Slightly flattened, it hangs crookedly.
It is fitting for the moon to be
imperfect today. Today in Nickel Mines,
the Plain Brethren are plowing
a new cornfield. The rows will be imperfect.

Still, ranks of blond-silked corn
will rise above blood-soaked roots—
above the disquieting remains
of a razed schoolhouse where little girls
were lined up . . . It is right that the
misshaped moon stand witness.

Farther on, I watch starlings rise and dip.
Their scratchy cursive falters
above the distant tree line and drops
into a branch-dark scribble . . .

> *The boys were freed.*
> *The door was blocked.*
> *Against the wall,*
> *the girls lined up.*

Some lines are impossible to translate.

The Leaving Season

for Mom, 1933-2008

It is the leaving season—
so why shouldn't the rains assail us,
borne as they are in weeping clouds
above the stubbled and forgotten fields?

Why shouldn't crook-backed trees
stagger under the weight of tears
pumped through the blue veins of leaves?

Why shouldn't the river flood,
disgorging bleached logs, clots of grass,
and the unrecognizable canker?

Why shouldn't geese assemble and grumble
as they knead the mothering marsh
one last time, or the hoary woodchuck sigh,
slipping into sleep?

We are all simple tenants here
and will each leave in our own way.
Even you—in this leaving season.

Funeral Procession

for Dad, 1925-2008

December is leafless, and the ridges
south of the Ohio reveal scars.
The snow resting on their flanks is dry
and airy. It slips off bony-shouldered
outcroppings like a thin blanket.

We are following the rail lines south.
The rail lines follow the river.
The river follows the curve of mountains.
The mountains are corded with veins of coal.

We drive into the coming night,
following our father home.
Lights flicker on in the coalfields.
Along the railroad tracks cracked coal,
as sharp as a man's dying, await loading.

I trace these mountains against my heart.
They are old and crook-backed, and
as knotted with sorrow as my father's hands.
I push my knuckles hard against my chest.
The night is saturated with sound—
the rasp of breath, the faded blanket rising
and then falling . . . and falling away.

You Can Have It Back

for Charleen Berels, 1951-2003

You can have it back—that which I borrowed,
or rather, which was borrowed on my behalf—this rib.
I never intended to keep it so long. Nor to bruise it.
See, there where the bone is soft? There where small fists
have pounded it as babes suckled.

I never intended to let it become so ravaged, so razored.
But I have birthed daughters, who slipped armored into
this world bearing arrowheads chipped from it.
And just today, as we buried a warrior it splintered—
hurtling a sliver inward. Forgive me; I never intended
to wear it so thin.

I should have treasured it more, or at least returned it sooner
since I could not keep it strong nor whole for you.
You can have it back now—this rib. I no longer need it
to hold me aright. And whether I should thank you
for the loan of it—I do not know. But I am grateful
for the sustenance it gave one winter when it was all I had
to gnaw upon.

Cerulean

What water molecules claim
are the long slow waves of light;
red, orange, green—pillaging
that which we cannot see.

Oh, but what is left behind!

Cerulean—
that quick pulse of blue,
the crystalline sapphire of the sky,
the immensity of aquamarine oceans.

Such blue—
like the cheekiness of chicory
       thrusting its blooms
       through the crumbling verge of the road.

It's there I'll go barefoot
to pick flowers for a house
where tears have stolen all the light.

In The Heart's Land

In the Heart's Land

There are no laws here in the land of the truly lost—
no vanishing point, no center, no periphery.
Latitude and longitude run parallel, and giggle about it.

I drift, unafraid, in this new topography, reveling
in a place of no gravity and no horizon.
Here shadows do not require a geography of memory
and circles are rarely perfect—but always naughty.

In the perfume of this place, I have no pulse.
There is no me, no you, no certainty in the process
of conversion. One inch equals the circumference
of a freckled stone or the speed of the Gulf Stream.

All points of reference have moved outward
in a silent and secret diaspora. And I am nameless
and happy here.

98.6 degrees was surpassed hours, or maybe eons ago.
In this place frostbite blossoms in the heat. In this place
birds and Sundays defy prevailing winds, and
the weather is always musical.

Here cartographers once stood and muttered of dragons.
Here the heart's land lies hidden in a capriciousness
that cannot be charted, nor plumbed, nor scaled.
Here magnetic north is a bogeyman's tale,
and the indigenous geography of snowlight
is my sole guide.

Love Poem for a Rainy Night

The storm has scuttled off, and evening boasts hoarded light—
a plumpsom swath of rose against sloe-berried blue.
And later still, an insolent moon. Ruddy-faced and drunk
on mossy wine, it whispers your name—one sinner to another.

January Morning

We curl on the white bed, buffeted by billowing down.
Cats purr, bowled in the swales. Your hand cups
the top of my head. Outside at the bird feeder,
my favorites—the juncos like little tufts of winter,
dusk gray above and drift white below—
retrieve grains of millet cast out by scrabbling jays.
And on the suet a red-capped downy positions himself
to pluck the fruit offered.

I sink my backside farther into the valley of your groin,
naturally seeking the heat. We do not speak. Later,
when coffee is made and the wood stove awakens
in the kitchen, we will talk of aging parents and errands,
and of who will layer on clothing against the skin-cracking
cold to seek the Sunday paper—snowed upon again.
Later still, we will surrender to the pinch of January's
cold fingers. You will search for the paper. I will fill the
feeder.

For now, we lie abed and watch the chickadees
and the cardinals. I think of the rough-legged hawk—
yesterday's surprise visitor. Banking past the roof,
his wing tip brushed the snow, tagging our house.
Then charcoal-feathered and smudge-headed, on a branch
above the pond he sat with his back to the feeder.

We were not fooled. His yellow glance read the comings
and goings of our winter lodgers; the field mice,
the mink from the wetland beyond the pasture,
the deer that sleep in the grass along the stream,
and our juncos—gray babushkaed and so plump.

Watching You Sleep

Your eyelids settle over the river
green mounds of your eyes. Stretched
out on a golden afternoon, our freckled limbs
entwined, I watch you sleeping. Miles
from melt water, miles from the loving cradle
of striated rock, I watch you dreaming. You—
surging across continents, feeling the rush
to contour mountains, to command ice,
to gouge valleys in the complacent soil.

Your eyes are river-green. Lying here with you,
I round a bend and find that I, too, am water—
the dark-eyed more deliberate sibling
dreaming of the pliant underbellies of loamy banks,
of diluvial secrets fingered by ghostly roots,
of the strider skimming across my skin.

Your eyes are river-green and flecked with hoarded gold.
Mine, the ocher of swallowed earth. I watch your head
on my breast, rise and fall. In sleep, you are heavier
than I imagined a favored son of the gods to be.

Marriage Bed

You sleep curled up,
one foot outside the blankets.
By the bed I stand,
bare feet on your blue shirt,
and watch the jealous snow
feign innocence against our window.

I will not wake you,
wanting, instead, what dreams
may linger unaware
in the heat of our bed—
in the cold clear morning of this room.

Reckonings

No, Not Lost

after Naomi Shihab Nye

What have you lost? the poet asks.
Nothing. Nothing at all, I say.
Except the ability to lose.

For example:
I have not lost the quiet panic of night's pacing,
nor the fading thunder of heartbeats I loved.

And certainly,
I've not lost the grimace of a friend
settling his dying into the sheets,

nor the molecules
that fling themselves wantonly
into the cosmos—and return—
with every tear I weep.

What have I lost?
Only the ability to lose.
For all these griefs, and more,
have been found in this brief and fragile life.

3.5 to 4 Percent

I rest on a coastal ridge.
It slopes steeply to the tidal silt
where mangroves elbow their way into the sea.

Far out, a flicker of fin—
seen, imagined, remembered—a reminder
you've sent of the muscular twitch
along the length of my spine,
of the salt that flows
through this body I carry about.

Your gray-blue turbulence
laps at the shore below me.
We are roughly equal in this burden of salt,
are each capricious in our own way, and
are both moon-benighted at the tidal pull
in our hearts.

When I rise to leave, you fling
dizzying memories at me.
Flaunt my ancient childhood—
finned and gilled—
in your lush and liquid care.
But I tell you, this child
is no longer yours.

Though the salinity of memory
surfaces at times, and I heed
the monthly tug of the moon, I know
my footprints are destined to fossilize
far from your bittersweet swell.

For it is this I have become—a daughter breached onto dust, a child of salt adrift beneath a desiccating sun.

A Life Bespoke

after Rachel Carson

Had there been a choice, would I have chosen
this arrangement of molecules, elements?
Why not a tree, a hunk of quartz,
or the tenacious barnacle clinging
in the tidal wrack? That would be a rhythmic
life—daily, nightly, the tides expected.
In between? Perhaps, ease.

Certainly not this constant waywardness,
nor the suspect step, nor the knowledge—
always in hindsight.

Who bespoke this ill-fitting life, anyway?
Who thought these arms and legs would know
what to do? Or this awkward heart?
In the night damp I twitch
to push *this,* that way. To pull *that,* this way.
To untangle the thread of base elements.

To cry: here carbon atom! Meet nitrogen, or oxygen,
or some other sibling hiding in the seams.
Go! Go off together. Become something.
Something fine and simple. Something that fits.

What I Bequeath

after Loren Eiseley

The voices are not illiterate.
In the night damp they rise—spawned mutterings
filtering from ancient fern forests, or crying out,
jellied, from alluvial stream beds.

I am reconciled to this misbegotten language—
the strangled gulps of ancestral gills,
the echo of doomed reptilian tread.

My footsteps in the tidal silt,
like calcified remains of wanderers before me,
foretell the delivery of a future fossil—a homecoming.

In some far time, shake the sand from white bones.
Know this was a life scripted of green twilight,
a voice scoured by the secretive river coursing
through cells that were once fin and fang.

And my bones will speak a language
yours can understand.

About the Author

Shutta Crum is an award-winning poet and children's book writer, as well as an oft-requested speaker and presenter at writing conferences, libraries, and schools. Her poems for adults have appeared in numerous small press publications and literary journals since the 1970s. That includes *Ann Arbor (W)rites, The Wayne Literary Review, The Huron River Review,* and *Writers Reading at Sweetwaters.* Over the years, she has placed in the top three finalists in several of the *Current Magazine* poetry competitions and was awarded first place in 2004. These days, a number of her poems appear in the *AAR2* (the online version of the *Ann Arbor Review*). She also has several children's books written in verse published by major publishers (Alfred A. Knopf, Clarion /Houghton Mifflin Harcourt, Albert Whitman, and Fitzhenry & Whiteside), as well as three novels. In 2005 she was invited to read at the White House, and in 2010 toured Japan presenting to the students of the Dept. of Defense schools.

WHEN YOU GET HERE brings some of Shutta's earlier published poems and many new poems together under one canopy.

Contact Shutta at:

Website ~ shutta.com

Facebook ~ facebook.com/Shuttacrum

Twitter ~ @Shutta

Instagram ~ instagram.com/Shuttacrum

Kelsay Books

Made in the USA
Monee, IL
08 March 2020